Audit Report

Report Number: OIG-SBLF-13-013

STATE SMALL BUSINESS CREDIT INITIATIVE: Kansas' Use of Federal Funds for Other Credit Support Programs

September 5, 2013

Office of Inspector General

Department of the Treasury

Contents

Results In Brief 2

Background 4

       The State of Kansas' Participation in SSBCI 5

       Kansas Capital Multiplier Loan Fund 5

       Kansas Capital Multiplier Venture Fund 6

Kansas Generally Used SSBCI Funds Appropriately, but May Have Exceeded the SSBCI Loan Limit 6

Kansas Did Not Obtain Complete Borrower and Lender Assurances at Loan Closing 9

Kansas Inaccurately Reported Funds Used By the Kansas Multiplier Loan Fund 11

Kansas Did Not Accurately Report Administrative Expenses or Use a Cost Allocation Plan for SSBCI-Related Audit Costs 12

Recommendations 14

Management Comments and OIG Response 14

Appendix 1: Objective, Scope, and Methodology 17

Appendix 2: Management Response 18

Appendix 3: Major Contributors 23

Appendix 4: Distribution List 24

Abbreviations

The Act	Small Business Jobs Act of 2010
CDC	Certified Development Company
National Standards	SSBCI National Standards for Compliance and Oversight
OCSP	Other Credit Support Program
OIG	Office of Inspector General
OMB	Office of Management and Budget
SSBCI	State Small Business Credit Initiative

OIG

The Department of the Treasury
Office of Inspector General

Audit Report

September 5, 2013

Don Graves, Jr.
Deputy Assistant Secretary for Small Business, Housing, and
   Community Development

This report presents the results of our audit of the state of Kansas' use of funds awarded under the State Small Business Credit Initiative (SSBCI), which was established by the Small Business Jobs Act of 2010 (The Act). Treasury awarded Kansas approximately $13.2 million[1] in SSBCI funding, and as of March 31, 2012, Kansas had received its first disbursement of approximately $4.3 million.[2] As of March 31, 2012, the state of Kansas had obligated or spent approximately $2.2 million[3] of the funds disbursed, of which approximately $1.5 million[4] was used by the Kansas Capital Multiplier Loan Fund, approximately $700,000[5] was used by the Kansas Capital Multiplier Venture Fund, and approximately $15,000[6] was for administrative expenses.

The Act requires the Treasury Office of Inspector General (OIG) to conduct audits of the use of funds made available under SSBCI and to identify any instances of reckless or intentional misuse. Treasury has defined reckless misuse as a use of allocated funds that the participating state or administering entity should have known was unauthorized or prohibited, and which is a highly unreasonable departure or willful disregard from the standards of ordinary care.

---

[1] Rounded up from $13,168,350.
[2] Rounded down from $4,345,556.
[3] Rounded down from $2,244,857.
[4] Rounded down from $1,533,322.
[5] Rounded up from $696,950.
[6] Rounded up from $14,585.

Intentional misuse is defined as a use of allocated funds that the participating state and or its administering entity knew was unauthorized or prohibited.

We contracted with TCBA Watson Rice LLP, an independent certified public accounting firm, to conduct the audit, which was performed from August 2012 to June 2013. The audit objective was to test participant compliance with program requirements and prohibitions to identify any reckless or intentional misuse of funds

To test participant compliance, the accounting firm reviewed all 11 loans and investments closed or obligated from the signing of the Allocation Agreement on June 28, 2011 to March 31, 2012. The accounting firm also reviewed the administrative expenses charged against the SSBCI funds as of June 30, 2012 to ensure they were allowable, reasonable, and allocable.

We conducted quality assurance procedures to ensure that the work performed by TCBA Watson Rice LLP was completed in accordance with *Government Auditing Standards*. We believe that the evidence obtained to address the audit objective provides a reasonable basis for the audit findings and conclusions. A more detailed description of our objective, scope, and methodology is in Appendix 1 of this report.

Results In Brief

Kansas appropriately used most of the SSBCI funds it had expended as of March 31, 2012. However, the Kansas Multiplier Loan Fund extended three $250,000 loans to affiliated entities as part of a $31 million aggregate financial arrangement. In doing so, the State may have exceeded the $20 million cap on SSBCI loans made under other credit support programs (OCSPs). Treasury's guidance does not address how the cap should be applied when funds are used to make companion loans comprising a larger financial package or where multiple loans are made to affiliated entities. Nevertheless, in the absence of clear guidance, the State should have sought clarification from Treasury.

The audit also disclosed that in each of the 11 transactions reviewed, Kansas did not obtain assurances from companion lenders that participated in the Kansas Capital Multiplier Loan Fund as required by *SSBCI Policy Guidelines* and *National Standards*. Also 5 of 11 assurances obtained from borrowers were not obtained prior to loan closing, as required. Treasury initially advised Kansas officials that due to the program's structure, the State was not required to obtain these assurances. The National Standards subsequently published by Treasury reversed this advice and required states to collect assurances from companion lenders. However, Treasury did not notify Kansas officials of the change.

Additionally, the State's March 31, 2012 *Quarterly Report* to Treasury inaccurately reported the amount of SSBCI capital that the Kansas Capital Multiplier Loan Fund had extended to businesses as it included a $173,822 advance to Network Kansas for administrative costs. While the $173,822 constituted funds used per Treasury guidance, the Kansas Capital Multiplier Loan Fund reported the used funds as a loan instead of administrative expenses. Kansas also understated administrative expenses on its June 30, 2012 *Quarterly Report* by $29,247. Of the funds not reported, $13,181 was used to pay audit and tax consulting fees for NetWork Kansas. These costs are not allowable as they had not been allocated through a cost allocation plan as required by OMB Circular A-87.

We recommend that Treasury clarify how the $20 million cap on credit extended by OCSPs should be applied to companion loans in a single financial arrangement and where multiple loans are made to affiliated parties. We also recommend that Treasury require Kansas to retroactively obtain lender assurances from the companion lenders that participated in existing Kansas Multiplier Loan Fund SSBCI transactions. Additionally, in all future transactions, Treasury should require the State to obtain lender assurances from its companion lenders. Further, we recommend that Treasury require Kansas to adjust the State's *Quarterly Reports* going forward to correct for inaccuracies in the March 31, 2012 and June 31, 2012 *Quarterly Reports* identified by the audit, determine whether a general event of default of the State's *Allocation Agreement* has occurred, and if so, take appropriate action. Finally, we recommend that Treasury disallow $13,181 in audit and tax consulting costs that were not properly allocated, ensure that such costs are excluded from the State's restated and subsequent *Quarterly Reports*, and require that Kansas provide a cost allocation plan or indirect cost proposal for administrative costs incurred by Network Kansas.

Treasury agreed to implement all of the recommendations, except for recommendation 2. Treasury stated it will direct the State to obtain lender assurances from relevant companion lenders in future transactions, but believes collecting them retroactively is impractical and unnecessary. The State has obtained assurances from the actual lenders, and has no contract or other relationship with companion lenders to form the basis for retroactively requesting the assurances. We agree with Treasury's response to recommendation 2 and believe that Treasury's planned actions are fully responsive to all of the recommendations. Formal written responses from Treasury and the state of Kansas are included in their entirety in Appendix 2.

Background

SSBCI is a $1.5 billion Treasury program that provides participating states, territories, and eligible municipalities with funds to strengthen Capital Access Programs and OCSPs that provide financial assistance to small businesses and manufacturers. Capital Access Programs provide portfolio insurance for business loans based on a separate loan loss reserve fund for each participating financial institution. OCSPs include collateral support, loan participation, loan guarantee, and venture capital programs.

Each participating state is required to designate specific departments, agencies, or political subdivisions to implement the programs approved for funding. The designated state entity distributes the SSBCI funds to various public and private institutions, which may include a subdivision of another state, a for-profit entity supervised by the state, or a non-profit entity supervised by the state. These entities use funds to make loans or provide credit access to small businesses.

Primary oversight of the use of SSBCI funds is the responsibility of each participating state. To ensure that funds are properly controlled and expended, the Act requires that Treasury execute an *Allocation Agreement* with each state, setting forth internal controls and compliance and reporting requirements before allocating SSBCI funds. SSBCI disbursements to states are made in three allocations: the first when the Secretary approves the state for participation, and the second and third after the state certifies that it has obligated, transferred, or spent at least 80 percent of the previous allocation. In addition, the participating state is required to annually certify that it has complied with program requirements.

The State of Kansas' Participation in SSBCI

On June 21, 2011, Treasury approved the State of Kansas as a participant in the SSBCI program, awarding it approximately $13.2 million. The *Allocation Agreement* between Treasury and the Kansas Department of Commerce was signed on June 28, 2011, authorizing use of the SSBCI funds for two new small business development programs: the Kansas Capital Multiplier Loan Program; and Kansas Capital Multiplier Venture Program. That same month, Treasury disbursed one-third of the State's allocation, approximately $4.3 million.

As of March 31, 2012, Kansas had obligated or spent approximately $2.2 million of the first disbursement, including approximately $15,000 for administrative expenses incurred for its two programs.

Kansas Capital Multiplier Loan Fund

The Kansas Capital Multiplier Loan Fund is administered by NetWork Kansas, a non-profit entity established in 2004, and provides matching funds through its partner network to eligible businesses in communities across Kansas. Entrepreneurs and existing small businesses access the Kansas Multiplier Loan Fund by working closely with local or regional financial institutions, NetWork Kansas partners, and angel investment networks. Businesses can apply for matching loans up to 9 percent of the private capital invested by financial institutions, Certified Development Companies (CDCs), and other sources of private lending.

Kansas Capital Multiplier Venture Fund

The Kansas Capital Multiplier Venture Fund is also administered by NetWork Kansas, and provides matching equity through its partner network to eligible businesses in Kansas communities. Similar to the Kansas Capital Multiplier Loan Fund, access to the Kansas Multiplier Venture Fund occurs through financial institutions, NetWork Kansas partners, and angel investment networks. Businesses can apply for matching equity up to 9 percent of the private equity invested. Private equity includes funds invested by private equity firms and angel investors. Eligible businesses include technology and bioscience companies working with a state entrepreneurial center, University Center of Excellence, and/or the Kansas Biosciences Authority. In addition, rural businesses or businesses in distressed areas of urban communities that meet specific criteria and are working with a NetWork Kansas partner may also qualify.

Kansas Generally Used SSBCI Funds Appropriately, but May Have Exceeded the SSBCI Loan Limit

We determined that the state of Kansas properly used the majority (64 percent) of the SSBCI funds it expended, and that 8 of the 11 transactions sampled were compliant with program guidelines related to prohibited relationships, maximum transaction amounts, use-of-proceeds, capital-at-risk, and other restrictions noted in the Act and *SSBCI Policy Guidelines*. However, we found that the State made three loans to affiliated entities as part of a larger financial arrangement with a family-owned limited liability company (the Company) that may have exceeded the $20 million SSBCI loan limit for OCSPs.

Specifically, the SSBCI-funded Kansas Multiplier Loan Fund extended three $250,000 companion loans to affiliated entities of the Company as part of a $31 million financial arrangement headed by a financial institution lender. The Company has operating facilities in several locations throughout Kansas.

In its application for financing, the Company cited the need to significantly expand its operations in order to meet the requirements of a new contract. To fill this expansion need, the Company presented plans to expand facilities, add production capacity, and obtain equipment for three of its operating facilities, each of which is owned by members of the family that owns the Company. The three operating facilities are located in different cities throughout Kansas and are organized as separate LLCs. As shown in Table 1, the resulting $31 million financial arrangement included several SSBCI loans that accompanied loans from the financial institution lender and the organization with which the Company has a new contract.

Table 1: Summary of Credit Support Extended to Affiliated Entities

	Loan Principal Amounts			
Source of Financing	Operating Facility 1 LLC	Operating Facility 2 LLC	Operating Facility 3 LLC	Total
Kansas Multiplier Loan Fund (SSBCI funds)	$250,000	$250,000	$250,000	$750,000
Financial Institution Lender				
Operating Loan 1	$3,650,000	$4,300,000	$3,798,000	$11,748,000
Operating Loan 2	$1,000,000	$1,000,000	$500,000	$2,500,000
Real Estate Loan	$7,753,069	$5,692,475	0	$13,445,544
Equipment Loan	$199,774	$944,463	0	$1,144,237
Organization Holding Production Contract	0	0	$1,097,788	$1,097,788
Total Financing	$12,852,843	$12,186,938	$5,645,788	$30,685,569

Source: The Company Application for Kansas Capital Multiplier Loan Funding

Although the Kansas Multiplier Loan Funds represented a small percentage of the aggregate financing extended to the Company, the funds were considered a necessary component of the project because the subordinate lien position provided the lending margins required for the loans made by the financial institution lender.

According to Section 3006(c) of the Act and Treasury's *SSBCI Policy Guidelines*, in order for a state OCSP to be eligible for SSBCI funds, the state must not, among other prohibitions, extend credit support to loans that exceed a principal amount of $20 million. The *SSBCI Policy Guidelines* further state that an OCSP cannot participate in an investment in which the resulting equity instrument is in excess of $20 million.

While the statutory loan limit and Treasury's guidance suggest that the amount of credit extended for a single loan should be capped at $20 million, it is unclear how to interpret the cap in the context of loans to affiliated entities or where the funds are used to make companion loans that comprise a larger financial package. On one hand, the State could be found compliant, because as noted in Table 1, the total financing extended separately to each LLC was under $20 million.

However, on the other hand, the loans could be viewed as constituting a single financing transaction benefiting one business entity) because:

- The overarching purpose of the loans was to expand the Company's operating capacity in order to meet the demands established by a new contract. Although each operating location is a unique LLC, all three LLCs are owned by varying compositions of family members that own the Company.

- Although separate applications for funding were submitted to the Kansas Multiplier Loan Fund for each of the three operating facility LLCs, the project information presented in each application was identical.

- The loans were cross-collateralized, contained cross-default provisions, and guaranteed by the owners of all three LLCs.

- The subordinate lien position provided the lending margins required for the loans made by the financial institution lender.

- The financial institution lender presented the terms and conditions for its loans to each of the operating facilities on the same date, August 31, 2011.

- The Kansas Multiplier Loan Fund awarded all three loans on the same day, November 10, 2011.

The State asserted it believed the transactions were compliant with the Act and *SSBCI Policy Guidelines* because the three operating facilities are separate LLCs, have different ownership structures, and are located in different geographic locations throughout Kansas. However, officials from the State said they did not seek approval or guidance from Treasury before commencing with these transactions.

Because the Act and *SSBCI Policy Guidelines* do not clearly address how the loan limit should be applied to companion loans comprising a larger financial package or to loans to affiliated entities, we did not find the Company loans to constitute a misuse of funds. However, given the unique nature of the financial arrangement, the State should have sought guidance from Treasury.

Due to the lack of clarity in the Act and *SSBCI Policy Guidelines*, Treasury will need to revise its guidelines to clarify how the $20 million cap on credit extended under OCSPs should be applied to companion loans in a single financial arrangement and to loans to affiliated parties.

Kansas Did Not Obtain Complete Borrower and Lender Assurances at Loan Closing

In each of the 11 transactions reviewed, Kansas did not obtain assurances from companion lenders that participated in the Kansas Multiplier Loan Fund, as required by the *SSBCI Policy Guidelines* and *National Standards for Compliance and Oversight* (*National Standards*). Additionally, 5 of 11 assurances obtained from borrowers were not obtained prior to loan closing, as also required by the *SSBCI Policy Guidelines*.

The *SSBCI Policy Guidelines* and the *National Standards* require that prior to the transfer of funds each state must obtain an assurance from the lender/investor affirming: (1) the loan or investment is not for a prior loan or investment that is not covered under the approved state program or that was owed to the borrower or investee or an affiliate of the lender or investor; (2) the loan or investment is not a refinancing of a loan or investment previously made to the borrower or investee by the lender or investor or an affiliate of the lender or investor; and (3) no principal of the lender or investor has been convicted of a sex offense against a minor.[7]

SSBCI Policy Guidelines also require that lenders and investors obtain borrower or investee assurances that: (1) loan or investment proceeds will be used for approved business purposes; (2) loan or investment proceeds will not be used for specifically prohibited purposes; (3) the borrower or investee and the lender or investor are not related parties; (4) the borrower or investee is not engaged in specifically prohibited activities; and (5) the principals of the borrower or investee have not been convicted of a sex offense against a minor.

The *National Standards* state that when a participating state makes a direct or companion loan under an approved direct loan or loan participation program, three use of proceeds forms must be executed: one by the borrower, one by the participating state, and one by the lender making the companion loan.

In December, 2011, Kansas officials sought clarification from Treasury regarding the applicability of the assurance requirement to the Kansas Capital Multiplier Loan Fund, specifically inquiring about whether assurances from companion loan lenders were required given the structure of the program. They explained that all of the program's funding arrangements are directed through CDCs, which provide the applicable assurances. The officials further noted that while private lenders may be involved on the matching side of a deal, the lenders do not benefit from SSBCI funding, and have no contractual relationship with the CDCs. In January, 2012, Treasury advised Kansas officials that they were not required to obtain assurances from financial institution lenders based upon the structure of the Capital Multiplier Loan Fund.

---

[7] The requirement that lender/investor assurances be obtained before the transfer of funds is set out in the *SSBCI National Standards for Compliance and Oversight*.

With the subsequent publication of the *National Standards*, Treasury's position on the subject changed. However, Treasury staff did not reach out individually to Kansas to discuss this change in policy. Therefore, Kansas officials proceeded as they had been previously advised.

NetWork Kansas officials also stated that borrower assurances were not obtained prior to loan closing on earlier transactions until participating partners referring transactions to NetWork Kansas became fully aware of the SSBCI programs requirements.

Under Section 6.1 of the State's *Allocation Agreement*, Treasury, in its sole discretion, may find a participant to be in default if the participant materially fails to comply with, meet, or perform any term, covenant, agreement, or other provision contained in the agreement. Because Kansas officials performed the necessary due diligence by requesting and then following Treasury's advice on lender assurances, we do not believe the missing assurances constitute an event of default of the State's *Allocation Agreement*.

However, in order to be in compliance with current policies, we recommend that Treasury require Kansas to retroactively obtain lender assurances from the companion lenders that participated in existing Kansas Multiplier Loan Fund SSBCI transactions. Additionally, in all future transactions, the State must obtain lender assurances from its companion lenders.

Kansas Inaccurately Reported Funds Used By the Kansas Multiplier Loan Fund

In its March 31, 2012, *SSBCI Quarterly Report*, Kansas misreported that the Kansas Capital Multiplier Loan Fund used approximately $1.5 million in allocated funds for loans. However, the reported amount included a $173,822 disbursement to NetWork Kansas for future administrative expenses. The *Allocation Agreement* and directions accompanying the *Quarterly Reports* define "allocated funds used" as those SSBCI funds that have been: (1) deposited with a lender to cover the Federal SSBCI contributions to a CAP reserve fund; (2) disbursed or committed to a specific borrower as part of a loan participation, collateral support, or direct lending program; (3) set aside to cover obligations arising from individual loan guarantees, loan participations, or collateral support agreements to specific borrowers; or (4) invested or committed to be invested in specific businesses, pursuant to a venture capital investment.

Kansas officials acknowledged the reporting error, and asserted it was the result of an accounting mistake. As a result of the error, the State's March 31, 2012 *Quarterly Report* was inaccurate by $173,822 in allocated funds used by the Kansas Capital Multiplier Loan Fund.

Reporting administrative costs as "allocated funds used for loans" overstates program performance and can distort the amount of funds obligated or spent, impacting decisions on state eligibility for additional disbursements. Treasury relies on the percentage of funds used in state *Quarterly Reports* to evaluate program effectiveness and to determine whether a state is eligible to receive additional allocations of its SSBCI award.

Therefore, Treasury should require that Kansas adjust its Quarterly Reports going forward to reflect the removal of $173,822 that was inaccurately reported in the March 31, 2012, *Quarterly Report* as allocated funds used by the Kansas Capital Multiplier Loan Fund. As a result of the reporting error, Treasury should determine whether a general event of default has occurred, and if such an event has occurred and not been adequately cured, whether future funding to Kansas should be suspended, reduced, or terminated. Finally, Treasury should require the State to demonstrate it has adequate accounting and reporting processes in place before approving additional disbursement requests.

Kansas Did Not Accurately Report Administrative Expenses or Use a Cost Allocation Plan for SSBCI-Related Audit Costs

NetWork Kansas disbursed $29,247 in SSBCI funds for administrative costs that was not reported on the State's June 30, 2012 *SSBCI Quarterly Report*. The $29,247 was not reported as administrative expenses because it had been rolled into the $173,822 that was incorrectly reported as a loan. As a result, Kansas will need to adjust the State's *Quarterly Reports* going forward to accurately reflect NetWork Kansas' use of SSBCI funds for program administration.

Additionally, $13,181 of its $29,247 was used to pay fees relating to the annual financial audit of Network Kansas and tax consulting fees, which were not properly allocated. NetWork Kansas, which administers multiple programs, did not allocate the cost of the audit to the SSBCI program through a cost allocation plan or indirect cost proposal as required by OMB Circular A-87.[8] Under OMB Circular A-87, audit costs required by, and performed in accordance with the Single Audit Act are allowable.[9] Other audit costs are also allowable if included in a cost allocation plan or indirect cost proposal, or if specifically approved by the awarding agency as a direct cost to an award. However, because the $13,181 was not properly allocated, it should be disallowed.

Because Kansas is not in compliance with OMB Circular A-87 and did not correctly report its administrative costs, it may be in general default of its *SSBCI Allocation Agreement.* Section 4.2 of that agreement states that the participating state shall use the allocated funds only for the purposes and activities specified in the agreement and for paying allowable costs of those purposes and activities in accordance with the cost principles set forth in OMB Circular A-87 and codified in 2 C.F.R part 225. If such an event has occurred and not been adequately cured, Treasury will need to determine whether future funding to Kansas should be suspended, reduced, or terminated.

Further, Treasury will need to ensure that the $13,181 associated with the audit and tax consulting costs are excluded from the State's adjustments of its *Quarterly Reports* going forward. It should also require that Network Kansas implement a cost allocation plan for administrative costs associated with the SSBCI program.

---

[8] OMB Circular A-87, *Cost Principles for State, Local, and Indian Tribal Governments.*
[9] The Single Audit Act was implemented by Circular A-133, "Audits of States, Local Governments, and Non-Profit Organizations."

Recommendations

We recommend that the Deputy Assistant Secretary for Small Business, Housing and Community Development:

1. Revise the *SSBCI Policy Guidelines* to clarify how the $20 million cap on credit extended by OCSPs should be applied to companion loans in a single financial arrangement and to multiple loans made to affiliated parties.

2. Require Kansas to retroactively obtain lender assurances from the companion lenders that participated in existing Kansas Multiplier Loan Fund SSBCI transactions, and inform the State that it is required to obtain lender assurances from its companion lenders in all future transactions.

3. Require Kansas to adjust the State's *Quarterly Reports* going forward to remove the $173,822 that was reported as a loan by the Kansas Capital Multiplier Loan Fund, and to add $29,247 in NetWork Kansas administrative costs that had not been previously reported, respectively.

4. Disallow the $13,181 in audit and tax consulting costs that were not properly allocated and ensure they are excluded from the State's restatement of its June 30, 2012 and subsequent *Quarterly Reports*.

5. Require the State to provide a cost allocation plan for administrative costs incurred by Network Kansas that is compliant with OMB Circular A-87.

Management Comments and OIG Response

We provided a draft of the report to Treasury on July 25, 2013, and received formal written comments on August 20, 2013 from Kansas and August 29, 2013 from Treasury. Treasury and Kansas agreed to implement all of the recommendations, except for recommendation 2.

In response to recommendation 2, Treasury agreed to direct the State to obtain the required lender assurances from relevant companion lenders in future transactions, but believes, like Kansas, that collecting them retroactively is impractical and unnecessary. The State has already obtained assurances from the actual lenders, and has no contract or other relationship with companion lenders to form the basis for retroactively requesting the assurances. Additionally, Treasury plans to clarify the *SSBCI National Standards for Compliance and Oversight* to specify which companion lenders must submit assurances.

Treasury stated it will revise the *SSBCI Policy Guidelines* to clarify the requirement that SSBCI funds not be used to support loans that exceed a principal amount of $20 million as proposed in recommendation 1. Regarding recommendations 3, 4, and 5, Treasury stated it will work with Kansas to correct its quarterly reports, remove $13,181 in disallowed audit and tax consulting costs from the State's quarterly reports, and review Network Kansas' cost allocation plan for administrative costs. Formal written responses from Treasury and the state of Kansas are included in their entirety in Appendix 2.

We agree with Treasury's response to recommendation 2, and believe that Treasury's planned actions are fully responsive to all of the recommendations.

* * * * * *

We appreciate the courtesies and cooperation provided to our staff during the evaluation. If you wish to discuss the report, you may contact me at (202) 622-1090, or Lisa DeAngelis, Audit Director, at (202) 927-5621.

/s/
Debra Ritt
Special Deputy Inspector General for
Office of Small Business Lending Fund Program Oversight

Appendix 1: Objective, Scope, and Methodology

We contracted with TCBA Watson Rice LLP, an independent certified public accounting firm, to conduct the audit, which was performed from August 2012 to June 2013. The audit objective was to test participant compliance with program requirements and prohibitions to identify any reckless or intentional misuse of funds.

To determine participant compliance the accounting firm tested all seven loans enrolled by the Kansas Capital Multiplier Loan Fund and all four investments enrolled by the Kansas Capital Multiplier Investment Fund from the signing of the Allocation Agreement on June 28, 2011, to March 31, 2012. The firm reviewed loan documentation for the loans sampled to determine whether Kansas complied with program requirements for prohibited relationships, maximum transaction amounts, use-of-proceeds, capital-at-risk, and other restrictions noted in the Act and *SSBCI Policy Guidelines*.

The accounting firm also reviewed the State's accounting procedures and quarterly reports for completeness, and interviewed Kansas officials who administer, account for, and report on SSBCI funding. The firm visited the offices of the Kansas Department of Commerce in Topeka, KS, and NetWork Kansas in Andover, KS to interview the management and staff responsible for administering, managing, accounting for the programs. Finally, the accounting firm reviewed the administrative expenses charged against the SSBCI funds to ensure they were allowable, reasonable, allocable, and adequately supported in accordance with Office of Management and Budget and *SSBCI Policy Guidelines*.

We conducted quality assurance procedures to ensure that the work performed by TCBA Watson Rice LLP was completed in accordance with *Government Auditing Standards*. Those standards require that the audit be planned and performed to obtain sufficient, appropriate evidence to provide a reasonable basis for our findings and conclusions based on our audit objective. We believe that the evidence obtained to address the audit objective provides a reasonable basis for the audit findings and conclusions.

Appendix 2: Management Response

DEPARTMENT OF THE TREASURY
WASHINGTON, D.C. 20220

August 29, 2013

Debra Ritt
Special Deputy Inspector General for
  Office of Small Business Lending Fund Program Oversight
U.S. Department of the Treasury
1500 Pennsylvania Avenue, NW
Washington, DC 20220

Dear Ms. Ritt:

Thank you for the opportunity to review the Office of the Inspector General's (OIG) draft report entitled *State Small Business Credit Initiative: Kansas' Use of Federal Funds for Other Credit Support Programs* (the Report). This letter provides the official response of the Department of the Treasury (Treasury).

We appreciate the Report's finding that Kansas generally used State Small Business Credit Initiative (SSBCI) funds appropriately. With your consent, Treasury transmitted a copy of the Report to Kansas program officials on July 30, 2013. Treasury asked Kansas to provide a narrative response describing the measures it has taken or plans to take to address the deficiencies noted in the Report.

In its reply, enclosed, Kansas states that the State appreciates the Report's findings and the opportunity to respond. Kansas disagrees with Recommendation 2 regarding obtaining companion lender assurances and provides three reasons that the State should not be required to retroactively obtain companion lender assurances under the Kansas Multiplier Fund. First, Treasury approved Kansas's process for collecting lender assurances. Second, since Kansas does not have a contractual relationship with the companion lenders and the companion lenders did not receive a direct benefit under the program, Kansas does not have any leverage to request or require the assurances. Third, since the direct lender under Kansas's program has already provided the assurances, collecting the same assurances from companion lenders is redundant.

Treasury accepts each of the Report's recommendations. With respect to Recommendation 1, Treasury will revise the *SSBCI Policy Guidelines* to clarify the requirement that SSBCI funds not be used to support loans that exceed a principal amount of $20 million. Regarding Recommendation 2, Treasury will inform Kansas that the State is required to obtain lender assurances from relevant companion lenders in future transactions, but agrees with Kansas that retroactively collecting companion lender assurances is impractical and unnecessary. Treasury plans to clarify the *SSBCI National Standards for Compliance and Oversight* to specify which companion lenders must submit assurances. Regarding Recommendations 3 through 5, Treasury will work with Kansas to correct its quarterly reports, remove the $13,181 in disallowed audit and tax consulting costs from the State's quarterly reports, and review Network Kansas' cost allocation plan for administrative costs.

Thank you once again for the opportunity to review the Report. Treasury appreciates our work together throughout the course of the SSBCI program.

Sincerely,

Don Graves
Deputy Assistant Secretary
Small Business, Community Development, and
Affordable Housing Policy

Enclosure

1000 S.W. Jackson St., Suite 100
Topeka, KS 66612-1354

Kansas
Department of Commerce

Phone: (785) 296-3481
Fax: (785) 296-5055 TTY: 711
admin@kansascommerce.com
KansasCommerce.com

Pat George, Secretary

Sam Brownback, Governor

August 20, 2013

CONFIDENTIAL

Don Graves, Jr.
Deputy Assistant Secretary
Small Business, Community Development and Affordable Housing Policy
Department of the Treasury
Washington, D.C. 20220

RE: State Small Business Credit Initiative: Kansas' Use of Federal Funds for Other Credit Support Programs

Dear Mr. Graves:

We have received the audit report (the Report) from the Office of Inspector General and appreciate the recommendations and opportunity to respond. The Kansas Department of Commerce (State) has already made significant improvements in several areas identified in the report. Below are our specific responses to the audit findings. We do have significant concerns over the Lender Assurances finding as will be more fully discussed below.

Finding #1
Did Kansas Exceed the $20 Million Cap on Other Credit Support Programs?

Kansas agrees with the Report that it generally used SSBCI funds appropriately and with an intent to meet the purpose of the program. With regard to the findings on the three separate $250,000 loans to separate legal entities, we contend these were not loans to a single "Company" as stated on pages 6-8 of the Report, but rather separate loans to separate legal entities. We believe the characterization that these loans were to a singular company is inaccurate and inconsistent with the overall finding on the issue.

SSBCI support for the three loans at issue were made to separate legal entities which were operated as separate businesses at separate locations, but who sold product to a common buyer. The loan structure was not contrived to avoid the $20M cap on loans. Each of the dairies has different controlling ownership and they function as separate businesses. While the similarity in names and inadvertent language in the applications make the independence of the loans more difficult to ascertain, review of the facts shows SSBCI loan support was not to a single loan in excess of $20M. Rather SSBCI funds were used to support separate loans to separate businesses.

Each of the LLC's operate independently, are separate legal entities and have separate controlling ownership. The principals share the same name and all produce high quality dairy product, which is neither uncommon in rural Kansas agriculture, nor surprising, given their exposure to successful dairy

Don Graves, Jr.
Small Business, Community Development and Affordable Housing Policy

operations. However, the LLC's each operate separately, have their own supplier contracts and sell their milk to a separately owned condensing plant prior to it being shipped to Texas. These entities were all created at separate times and, factually and legally, could not have been structured to take advantage of the SSBCI program. Simply sharing a common contract to provide product to a single buyer, should not result in these loans as being characterized as a single loan. Consequently, we believe the reference to a singular "Company" or the loan beneficiary is misleading.

Finding #2
Did Commerce Obtain Appropriate Borrower and Lender Assurances?

Kansas strongly disagrees with the finding it failed to comply with SSBCI requirement regarding the assurances that must be obtained from "lenders". In particular, given that Kansas has no privity of contract or other relationship with the banks who made these companion loans, the recommendation that Kansas obtain these assurances on a retroactive basis is completely impracticable. Simply put, there is no legal or other relationship between those banks and Kansas' SSBCI program to form the basis for such a request. All parties, NetWork Kansas, the Borrower and the certified development company (CDC) have signed the assurances. Getting the assurances document from another party is redundant.

As noted in the Report, Kansas has a unique program structure and received approval of its process from Treasury and authorization to obtain the assurances from the CDC's who are the actual lenders for the Kansas program in January 2012. Kansas relied on that approval from Treasury to continue the program structure agreed to by Kansas and Treasury, which is outlined in Kansas' grant application as well as its Allocation Agreement. Kansas has complied with the National Standards by obtaining assurances from each of the lenders (the CDC's) under its program. Because of the written confirmation from Treasury that Kansas was operating the program in compliance with SSBCI requirements, there is no legal basis to ask the state to go back retroactively and seek those assurances from companion lenders with whom Kansas has absolutely no relationship, no legal basis to request or ability to enforce a refusal to sign the assurances document.

Kansas believes it is in compliance with the National Standards because the companion lenders receive no direct benefit from SSBCI funds and never have access to or get loan support from the SSBCI funds. Kansas has implemented a program change to insure Borrower assurances are obtained prior to closing.

Finding #3
Kansas Inaccurately Reported Funds Used by the Kansas Multiplier Loan Fund.

Kansas accepts the finding that it erroneously reported use of certain allocated funds. Once the audit process is complete, Kansas will adjust its Quarterly Reports to reflect removal of the $173,822 that was inaccurately reported on the March 31, 2012 Quarterly Report. The state has put procedures into place that will prevent any similar issues in the future.

Don Graves, Jr.
Small Business, Community Development and Affordable Housing Policy

Finding #4 and #5
Kansas Did Not Accurately Report Administrative Expenses or Use a Cost Allocation Plan for SSBCI-Related Audit Costs.

Kansas also accepts the findings related to reporting of administrative costs and the cost allocation plan for SSBCI related audit costs. The state has adjusted its Quarterly Reports going forward to better reflect use of the program funds for program administration. Kansas has also accepted from NetWork Kansas a cost allocation plan for any administrative costs associated with the SSBCI program. That cost allocation plan will insure that costs are allowable and properly allocated in conformance with OMB Circular A-87. A copy of the plan will be provided to Treasury under separate cover.

We appreciate the professionalism of the audit team and the opportunity to provide this management response.

Sincerely,

Pat George
Secretary

cc: Debra Ritt,
Special Deputy Inspector General for Office of Small Business Lending Fund Program Oversight
Jamie Lipsey, Department of Treasury

Appendix 3: Major Contributors

Debra Ritt, Special Deputy Inspector General

Clayton Boyce, Audit Director

Lisa DeAngelis, Audit Director

John Rizek, Audit Manager

Andrew Morgan, Auditor-in-Charge

Safal Bhattarai, Auditor

Joe Berman, Referencer

Appendix 4: Distribution List

Department of the Treasury

Deputy Secretary
Office of Strategic Planning and Performance Management
Risk and Control Group

Office of Management and Budget

OIG Budget Examiner

United States Senate

Chairman and Ranking Member
Committee on Small Business and Entrepreneurship

Chairman and Ranking Member
Committee on Finance

Chairman and Ranking Member
Committee on Banking, Housing, and Urban Affairs

Chairman and Ranking Member
Committee on Homeland Security and Governmental Affairs

Chairman and Ranking Member
Appropriations Subcommittee on Financial Services and General Government

United States House of Representatives

Chairman and Ranking Member
Committee on Small Business

Chairman and Ranking Member
Committee on Financial Services

Chairman and Ranking Member
Committee on Oversight and Government Reform

Chairman and Ranking Member
Appropriations Subcommittee on Financial Services and General Government

Government Accountability Office

Comptroller General of the United States

www.ingramcontent.com/pod-product-compliance
Lightning Source LLC
Chambersburg PA
CBHW081820170526
45167CB00008B/3479